Let Me Tell You…

the journey from my darkest night to a stormy night when fear was replaced by lasting peace.

Childhood Memories
of World War II
by

Edmund Spieker

Copyright © 2012 by Edmund Spieker
Illustrations by Marcia d'Haese
Book design and layout by Gravitation Studios

ISBN 978-1-4675-1549-8

All rights reserved. No part of this work may be reproduced or copied in any form or by any means–graphic, electronic, or mechanical including photocopying, recording, taping, or information and retrieval systems – without written permission of the author.

Gravitation Studios Publishing
Raleigh, North Carolina

Printed in the United States of America

Dedication

I am serious by nature and don't laugh easily. Maybe it's because of the traumatic experiences of World War II with its horrors, destruction, death and the long flight from the invading armies paired with hunger and sickness. But it could also be just something I inherited from my father. My mother and his family described him as a man of character with a deep faith, serious and loyal. I saw him for the last time when I was 5 years old. He was given a leave of absence and stayed with us for a few days before returning to the battle lines in Russia. It was the last time we saw him. A few weeks later he was listed as "missing in action." He was part of the 12th tank division that disintegrated on the east front. We never again heard of him. Neither the Red Cross nor any other search organization could inform us of his whereabouts.

My mother was a very sensitive and humble person. Her faith was simple and profound. The problems and challenges of life drove her into the arms of her Savior Jesus, whom she received when she was only five years old. She loved my father very much and never considered marrying again. She kept his image alive in our minds when she would tell us about him as a man with a deep commitment for God and family. Even growing up without the physical presence of my father, I always knew what the qualities of real man are and what would make him proud of me.

I can't imagine better parents than mine. Their lives were the best example; and their genuine faith was the greatest legacy. It is with profound love and gratitude that I dedicate to them this simple account of my remembrances of World War II.

Edmund Spieker

Cary, NC
January 2012

About the Author

Edmund Spieker was born in Witten/Ruhr West Germany a few months before the start of World War II. While his father was drafted into the war in 1943, his mother along with the children were evacuated to the Sudetenland, part of the Czech Republic which belonged to Germany before World War I. That is where the flight started in May 1945.

Edmund tells the story of their flight from Sudetenland back to West Germany as truthful as he remembers, and as "Mutti" his dear mother had rehearsed it many times after the war.

In 2007, Edmund was able to return to Teplitz Schoenau (now Tepliza) in the Czech Republic. Even though he knew only the name of the street where they had lived before their flight started, he was able to locate the school where he and his brother, Dieter, had attended and the hospital where Ursula, his sister, was born. For many years, he had dreamed to revisit the same spot where his longest wait ever had occurred (see Chapter 2).

Edmund often told his stories to his grandchildren. It was Katrina Scheiern, his grandchild, who would get so excited about hearing them. In fact, when her class studied the history of WWII at Cary Christian School, she convinced her teacher, Mrs. Manchester, that her Grandpa should be invited to tell his story to the kids at school.

This is how it started. Here are the first articles. Mr. Spieker wishes for these stories to inspire many kids to better understand the complexities of war and life, but especially the reality of God's presence with those who fear Him.

Edmund and his wife, Marli, reside in Cary, NC. Both are active in missionary work. Marli is the global ministry director of Project Hannah, a ministry of Trans World Radio. Edmund works with Churches in Missions, and besides coordinating Short-Term Mission trips he also leads Pastor Care Clinics in Brazil and other countries.

Let me tell you…

CHAPTER 1
About the Darkest Night. 9

CHAPTER 2
About the Longest Wait Ever. 13

CHAPTER 3
About the Great Confusion. 17

CHAPTER 4
Of an Unforgettable Birthday. 21

CHAPTER 5
How We Survived in the Midst of the Enemy. . . . 25

CHAPTER 6
Of Angels Unaware. 29

CHAPTER 7
How We Crossed the Border. 33

CHAPTER 8
How We Made It Home. 37

CHAPTER 9
About Mutti's Unconditional Love. 41

CHAPTER 10
How God Prepared Us for the Unbelievable. 45

CHAPTER 11
About the Great Discovery. 49

CHAPTER 12
About a Stormy Night. 53

Let me tell you…

About the Darkest Night

I was shivering. The fact that there were at least 15 of us packed into the small cellar made no difference. Besides the cold humidity of that dreary place, with its smell of old and rotten potatoes, there was fear and high tension in the air. The voices were hushed as if the pilots of the airplanes we were expecting could hear us. When the siren from the neighboring school building sounded the shrill "Vollalarm," the last flickering candle light was extinguished. We were in yet another air raid. In seconds, we could hear them…

Chapter 1

first like humming bees, but soon with the roar of hundreds of engines; the enemy was upon us.

My sister, Marlene and I were pressed together, our heads buried in my mother's lap. Mutti (German for mommy or mother) was holding baby Ursula in one arm while the other embraced the oldest of us four children, Dieter, my brother. Would we survive this time? Her lips were moving in a silent prayer to the God she knew and trusted wholeheartedly. "Lord Jesus, thank you for being with us. Whatever will happen you know best. Please protect us from the evil one," prayed Mutti.

It was April 1945. The nightmare of World War II had started almost six years earlier. Like a wild and indomitable beast, the war was killing thousands of lives every day. Not only soldiers on the front lines but also the civilian population in industrialized cities were its constant victims. To escape those horrible bombardments in the Ruhrgebiet, one of Germany's most important industrial parks, our family had been evacuated to the Sudetenland, part of the old German territories Hitler had annexed to the Third Reich.

For months, the Russian army was forcing the German Wehrmacht (army) to retreat, so the battle front was coming closer and closer to us. Our house was right on the main street, where soldiers and armament were moving in one direction while refugees and the wounded moved in the opposite direction. There was no important industry in our area, but the allied bombardments had become more regular and served the purpose to weaken any resistance that was left.

After living for a while with the constant possibility of nightly air raids, one should become used to being awakened in one's best sleep, to put on one's clothes and to run to the basement. But nothing could be further from the truth for me. My sleep was deep and heavy. Unfortunately, I was of no help to my dear mother who had to mobilize us four children: Dieter (8), Edmund (almost 6), Marlene (4) and Ursula (6 months).

I still remember Mutti's kind and loving voice, "Edmund, komm doch, zieh den Strumpf an." (Edmund, please come and put on your socks). How could I? My eyes wouldn't stay open and my whole body screamed for more sleep. Those airplanes didn't know me and how could their bombs ever hit us? So after Mutti had finally put on one sock and placed the other in my hands to dress the next foot, I didn't know better and dropped the one she gave me while pulling off the other one already on. She never lost her temper. Always kind and, yes, firm, she finally got us to the basement.

And that is where we were that night waiting for the bombs to fall. Only seconds after the first airplanes roared over us we heard a rapidly increasing whistle descend from heaven. We recognized the sound and knew the bombs were raining down. There was no escape. Everyone was paralyzed with fear. Then, the terrible impact…the walls were shaking as the bomb exploded. A neighboring house had been hit. It wasn't long, before we heard the sirens of the fire truck.

But the bombardment continued. The dark, cold and terrible night wasn't over yet. Hundreds of airplanes were flying over us in formation. We were lucky that they were clumsy and heading only one direction while unloading their deadly cargo over the sleeping cities on the way.

Finally, the frightening roar of those enemy airplanes ebbed away. Soon the siren howled the "Endalarm." As the lights came on, new hope and relief flickered on the pale faces. We had been spared one more time. In a hurry, we climbed the stairs to our apartment where Mutti, with a prayer of thanks, lovingly tucked us into bed. For me, it was the end of the darkest night I remembered.

Let me tell you…

About the Longest Wait Ever

"Please don't get my sister-in-law all nervous. If the Russians were coming, I would know!"…Uncle Ernst was calming our neighbor who had stormed into our kitchen blurting out the news that the Russian army was advancing and that all Germans had to leave town immediately. Uncle Ernst had dropped in for a short visit from a nearby army post to encourage my mother. I liked him very much. He was the youngest brother of my father who had just been listed as "missing in action" on the east front. Uncle Ernst was fun and always so assuring in his impressive uniform. I trusted him fully. As a German officer, he definitely should know best. As he was leaving he told my mother, "Magdalena, if you really need to leave, I will come and pick up you and the children. We have a couple of trucks at the army post. Don't worry."

We knew for weeks that the front was coming closer. Day and night we could hear the thundering of the cannons. There was a constant movement of soldiers and armored vehicles on the street. One day a long line of bicycles, with about 50 boys ages 12 years and up belonging to the "Wehrwolf," a Hitler youth group, advanced east with a "Panzerfaust" (bazooka) over their shoulders. Small attack planes were now surprising us regularly. One time, Dieter had been the target as he was crossing a nearby soccer field. The pilot had pursued him with machine gun fire. He only escaped because he threw himself in a ditch.

The tension of war was in the air. It's no wonder that Uncle Ernst wanted to calm the fears of my mother. She was already deeply burdened with the bad news that my father was missing in action. And then, how could she ever escape with her four small children unless she got a ride?

As the door closed after Uncle Ernst, Mutti turned on the radio. It wasn't news time yet but she needed to know. Then, right after the first crackles of the 'Volksempfaenger' (Peoples Radio), there it was: "Achtung! Achtung! Alle deutschen Einwohner muessen sofort Teplitz Schoenau raeumen! Die Russen kommen!" (Attention! Attention! All German citizens must leave Teplitz Schoenau immediately! The Russians are coming!") – "Run after Uncle Ernst…" my mother shouted to Dieter. And run he did. Dieter was fast, but not fast enough. He just saw Uncle Ernst's car turn the curb and… he was gone. Too late! What now? Mutti decided to wait.

What happened next was close to chaos. In a matter of minutes, the street was filled with vehicles and people, some running, others shouting. Horns were honking as cars were trying to find their way through the throng of people with hand wagons and on bicycles. All were moving west, in the direction of the German homeland.

Only half a block away from our house was the school Dieter and I attended. With the battle lines approaching, it had been transformed into an emergency hospital, a "Lazarett," for wounded soldiers. We had become accustomed to playing during recess between the soldiers who were recovering from their surgeries. Now, with the news that the Russians were coming, soldiers who could already walk left the building in droves. I will never forget the soldier whose left leg had been amputated. He was still bleeding through the bandages as he hobbled on his crutches. He stopped to speak to Mutti who had opened the window, which was directly on the sidewalk to watch the unfolding stampede. – "Lady, run for your life. The Russian soldiers are animals who spare no woman. Take your children and escape!" he warned my mother. We knew he meant well. But how could we run? Uncle Ernst would soon be here.

As the hours passed by, the street became more deserted. We were still waiting and watching. I looked intensely toward the east, the direction where Uncle Ernst's car had disappeared. At one time when we came in to report to Mutti, the neighbor who lived in the attic above us stumbled through the main entrance. He was totally drunk and now trying to get up the stairs. Other men were helping him. I can't remember who told me that he was a Czech and had been an informant to the occupying German forces. He was desperate and knew that he had nothing good to expect from the Russians.

I went back outside and stood there for a long time looking down the street in the direction where we expected Uncle Ernst's car or maybe truck to appear. To the left of the street was the huge school building. To the right side was a row of houses; and further down, after the curb in the road the hospital, where my little sister, Ursula, had been born. But with the falling darkness, our hope disappeared. By now, the streets were deserted. Uncle Ernst had not come. I had never waited with such high expectancy for anything; and it definitely was for me, at almost 6 years old, the longest wait ever.

Let me tell you…
About the Great Confusion

"Mutti, what happened?" I was always deeply moved when mother was crying. And there were more reasons than enough to be sad and desperate in those last days of World War II.

It was April 30, 1945. The radio had just announced the death of the German Fuehrer (leader) Adolf Hitler. Unbelievable! He had promised to usher in a millennium of peace and prosperity for a new world. Only 10 days earlier we had celebrated his 56th birthday with many flags and a lot of "Marschmusik." The war was at a crisis point and everybody knew that the new "Wunderwaffe" (wonder weapon) would soon bring the long expected victory over those enemies who where bombarding us day and night. With a somber voice, the radio announcer explained how the Fuehrer had given his life among his beloved soldiers on the east front. How was that possible? No wonder Mutti was crying. That was the worst news anyone could have ever expected.

As almost any German citizen in those days, she too believed in the just cause of the war. The radio had been telling us about it every day all day long for the last six years. Even my father, who was a fine Christian, left home not yet fully recovered from his wounds because he felt obligated to be at the side of his comrades who were fighting the advancing Russian army. At the same time he had actually told Mutti that he was sure that there would be no place for Christian faith in Germany if the Nazi party would continue to rule.

A few weeks earlier, a lady from the party had paid us an unexpected visit. She walked into our kitchen with a harsh "Heil Hitler" (Save Hitler) demanding the name and age of each of us boys. When mother asked what this was for, the lady responded that we were old enough to participate in the pre-Hitler youth. My mother had learned from the Lutheran pastor what a group of rowdies those Hitler-Youth were, and she resisted. "God entrusted these children to my care. I will not let them go," said Mutti… "What, you are a German mother and have the audacity to resist our orders?" responded the lady. And then mother said humbly, but plainly, "One can only serve God or the devil." She didn't want to offend the lady nor speak against the government. She was only reacting with motherly care due to what she had learned about those wild and disrespectful youngsters. But it was too much. The lady from the party was livid as she stormed out of the room. She turned at the door and spit out with hate, "We will talk again soon." And then she was gone. Mutti didn't know what to do about that. There were so many contradictory factors; and people were afraid to question anything. Why was everybody so cross and why all the hatred and killing?

A few weeks earlier my father had been declared as "missing in action" on the Russian front and now Hitler was dead! What would become of Germany and all the dreams for a better world? Everything seemed lost and hopeless. Mother knew she could not stay in Teplitz Schoenau, Sudetenland. She had to go back home to Luetgendortmund, Westfalen. But, how?

Less than a week later, the flight began. The day the order was given to evacuate the city, we waited in vain for Uncle Ernst to return and pick us up. The next day, mother and the four of us (Ursula in her carriage) were standing beside the road, hoping that one of the retreating army vehicles would grant us a ride. Suddenly, two "Panzerspaehwagen" (armored vehicles) stopped. The leading officer shouted, "Lady, where are you heading to?" "Ruhrgebiet," Mutti answered. "Hop on!" She with little Ursula and Dieter climbed with the small bag and folded carriage in the first vehicle, and my sister, Marlene, and I were helped into the second car and off we went. The soldiers were friendly. They too were from the Ruhrgebiet. We didn't mind that they were SS troops.

As we left town and approached the open road suddenly Russian airplanes dove from the sky to attack our convoy with machine gun fire. Our driver was shot in the heart. Marlene and I were sitting in the back of the vehicle but couldn't see the details. Another soldier took the steering wheel.

After a while we stopped again. This time the leading vehicle had a flat tire. The street was blocked. The bridge before us had been blown up.

How could we continue? The soldiers listened to their radio for the latest communication. "The Americans stopped again; the Russians will be here tomorrow," said one of them. "We won't make it!" There was silence. Then, the leading officer told my mother to move on. "If the Russians find you with us you will also be killed. But do us a favor," he said. He handed Mutti a sheet of paper containing the names and addresses of the whole group. "Pass our greetings to our families," he said. But then, as we were walking away to the nearby town he called Mutti back. "Please return the list; we don't want our families to know that we were so close to home and had to die." How sad! What a waste! Where had all the hysteria of war taken us? There was nothing mother could do. Her heart was heavy as we walked away. Everything was so confusing and hopeless.

Let me tell you…

Of an Unforgettable Birthday

Spring was in the air. The trees and flowers were blossoming in their beautiful colors. Thousands of birds had just arrived from their winter retreat in the warmth of southern Europe and filled the air with their twitter and singing. Best of all, May 10th was my sixth birthday. Mutti knew how to throw a surprise. She loved to celebrate every special event with beautiful decorations and singing. But would today be any different?

Chapter 4

We had found refuge in the second floor classroom of a school building the night before in the city of Zaaz. There were no beds to sleep on and no cover to keep us warm. But because it was also the hide-out of young German soldiers, there was a lot of straw to use for sleeping. And they had food, yes, food! I was starving! They shared their beef rations with us. One of them gave me his pocket knife as a gift. I remember him telling my mom that they would hide their ammunition boxes right under the straw and pick them up later, after the war was over. The next morning, they were all gone.

It was then that mother gave me my birthday gift. Today, the maximum she could afford was a piece of square sugar and a hearty birthday kiss. She said next time we would celebrate my birthday with cake and candles. In her loving way she told me that she was proud of me. She assured me that the Lord Jesus would help us all on our way back home. I was fine with that and proudly showed her that fancy army knife the soldier had given me. She didn't seem too happy with that: "Edmund, so sorry, but you cannot keep this." "Why not? " I said. "It has the Hitler eagle engraved in the handle and that would make the Russians very angry." said Mutti. But I was not ready to give up so easily. But Mutti insisted, and I knew deep in my heart that she was right. I couldn't keep it and finally gave it to her. That was the end of my knife.

From our window, we could see how people were fixing white bed linen on their windowsills which waved in the wind like flags. Mother explained that it was supposed to be a sign of peace and a welcome to the Russian army due to arrive anytime. Young ladies and beautifully dressed girls holding flowers in their hands were lining the streets as if to welcome the victors. Mother told us that those were Czech people who were not fond of the Germans.

It was about noon, when the first Russian soldier appeared on a motor-bike. I observed it from behind the closed window. A few moments later other motorbikes followed, then tanks, and soon the Russian troops. We had been over rolled by the enemy forces.

I don't remember all what happened next. But I clearly remember hearing the screaming of women during the night. At one point, there were loud and angry voices in the stairwell. Two drunken Russian soldiers wanted to come up the stairs because they insisted that they had seen a "matka" (woman) in the window. The friendly janitor who had given us refuge in the school tried hard to hold them back. He was Czech but also spoke Russian and wanted to protect us. While the discussion went on, Mutti signaled for us to be quiet as she soundlessly slipped away to hide on the next floor. Finally, the racket was over. We heard a door slamming shut. Our friend had been able to convince the drunken soldiers to leave, and they left in anger and with much noise.

After a while Mutti came back still shivering with fear but so thankful that once more God had protected us. As she tried to put us to sleep, I knew that I would never forget my sixth birthday.

Let me tell you…

How We Survived in the Midst of the Enemy

It was still dark when Mutti woke us up. In no time we were ready. There were no clothes to change. All we had was in a little suitcase and most of that belonged to baby sister, Ursula. Mutti held Ursula in one arm and my sister Marlene on the other hand. Dieter carried her foldable carriage while I followed with the small suitcase down the stairs. Quietly, we stepped outside the school building that had been our first hiding place. Mutti turned onto the next street and instructed us to stay close to her and to bow down whenever we passed houses where the light was shining through the windows. Nobody should see us since it was still curfew time, and we were fleeing the city to get to West Germany.

Finally, we stopped at a house and Mutti knocked softly on the door. It opened slightly. When the lady recognized mother, she waved us in. Her family was also ready to leave. I learned that if we made it to the train station in time we might be able to catch a ride to the West. In no time, we were back on the dark street. Nobody spoke as we headed toward the train station.

When we finally arrived there, the sun was rising. The platform was filled with people who also were waiting for the train. It should be arriving at any time. Suddenly, a lady approached Mutti. She had been looking in our direction before and now finally found the courage to talk to her. "Are you Frau Spieker?" she asked Mutti.…"Yes, I am," Mutti answered. "But,… but,…you should be in the concentration camp, and here you are well and alive!" she said. Mutti didn't know what to say. "Yes here I am and alive, but why not?" Suddenly, she remembered the threat of the lady from the party that wanted us boys for the pre-Hitler youth. Unbelievable! What kind of people were these? The whistle of the train entering the station interrupted any further conversation. Now, we had to find a way to get onto it.

I can't remember the details of how we made it on the train but I remember clearly that we had to get off not very long after and wait for another train at a bigger station. I can still see that station in my mind but the seriousness of what happened there I know from Mutti herself. It was a sunny day. While we were waiting for our train, we children walked and played around the piles of ammunition that were sitting right in the midst of the platform. Suddenly, a Russian officer approached Mutti and barked in broken German, "You come with me…my room!" Mutti was horrified and screamed, "Never, never… Cut my throat first!" He gripped little Ursula's carriage and walked with her in the direction of the station building. Mutti stood paralyzed. She was crying in her heart for help from above. At that very moment Marlene who had tried to climb onto a freight car fell down and started screaming from the top of her lungs. Mutti knew this was the answer. As she ran to assist Marlene, she shouted to Dieter to get the carriage with Ursula from the Russian. She was safe. The Russian let go, and thank God the next train arrived just in time.

Trains were rare in those days after the chaos of war. There was no published time table. If they ran, people would fill every inch inside, and also climb and hang onto the outside. Twelve million Germans were displaced after the war. One can only imagine the extent of the crisis as there was a shortage of food, and a total breakdown in communications, transportation and governmental services. But Mutti had to get her four children back to safety, and that meant always being on the lookout for some way to get closer to her target, the Ruhrgebiet in West Germany.

We took another train which was a combination of freight and passenger wagons; and only through God's grace were we able to get into one of the passenger compartments. But the terror started when that train ended up stuck in an open field not far from a city and didn't move for another four weeks. I can still see in my mind the place where we fetched water and the improvised places set up to wash clothes. People would extend lines to dry them in the sun. I don't remember where the food came from, but I know that there was never enough. Hunger was a constant companion. But the worst of all were the nightly assaults by Russian soldiers who would come and brutalize the women. Sometimes I wonder how God protected me from becoming traumatized with all of the commotion and screaming that was common place every night. Mutti was wearing my Dad's pants and several layers of clothes since that was the only way to keep them. The lack of food and the constant concern and care for us four small children had taken its toll. She was only 33 years old, but she was pale and she looked old and sick. In the dark of the night, when the Russians shined their flashlight through the door of our compartment they were quick to say "Matka krank" (Woman sick)… and they left her in peace. Without realizing it at the time, that was another example of God's protection for us in midst of our enemies.

Let me tell you...

Of Angels Unaware

"**M**ein Gott!" (my God) was one of those expressions I remember most from those dark and hopeless days of our flight. It was as if people were appealing to the Almighty to help them understand and deal with so many terrible things. Millions of Germans who had been driven out of their homelands were fleeing like us and seeking refuge somewhere. In order to get them off the streets, the occupying forces jailed them in improvised refugee camps. We, too, ended up on a school property right in the center of the town of Chemnitz together with hundreds of people, mostly women and children. There, the women shocked each other with their horrendous stories of suffering, loss and death; I often heard them saying "Mein Gott!"

But what did God have to do with the horrors of the Nazi regime or now with the brutality of the occupying forces? What was His involvement in the war? Did He see the terrible bombings that for years, night after night had killed thousands upon thousands of innocent children and civilians? Was He interested in caring for us now that we were homeless, sick and starving?

I was too young to ponder those questions, and my mother didn't seem to entertain those thoughts. On the contrary, her God was always a close friend and constant companion. She knew that no evil would come from Him. She kept at peace in the midst of chaos, and when she prayed with us, we knew that we could hope for a better tomorrow. She told the Lord about our plight and humbly asked Him to provide. And God answered her prayers through angels unaware.

The school property that served as our refugee camp was surrounded by barbed wire. Dieter, my older brother, had found a hole in the fence, and he had gotten through it. As he was standing on the sidewalk, a Russian soldier stopped his bicycle right in front of him and ordered that he take care of the bike. He then went into a store on the other side of the street. It took a while until the Russian came back. As he took the bike from Dieter, he handed him a bill of 10 Reichsmark. That was good money. Dieter ran to Mutti and now she was able to buy us some food. Amazing! But could a Russian soldier qualify as an angel unaware?

The sanitary conditions in that refugee camp were terrible. There was no place to shower or to take a bath. We had to sleep with about 30 people on the floor in one classroom. During the night, vermin, disease carrying flies and lice, plagued us. Once a day, we received a food ration consisting of a watery Rutabaga soup that had no taste and contained no protein. I remember us standing in long lines with our old pots and cans. People would joke saying that there were more eyes looking at the soup then swimming in the soup. But at least it was warm and edible, but never enough to still the hunger.

One late afternoon a young lady standing on the sidewalk outside the fence called to my sister, Marlene. She offered to take her into her home. In spite of her 4 ½ years, Marlene was a model of obedience and knew that she should not go with strangers. She ran to Mutti and told her about the invitation. My mother spoke with the young lady and then called me to accompany my sister. We followed the young lady across the street. The house she was living in had survived the bombardments. They lived on the second floor. I still remember entering that apartment. The light seemed so bright and everything so astonishingly beautiful.

First, we were taken to the bathroom and given a bath. What a delight after so many weeks! They also washed some of our clothes and dried them on the warm oven. Then, we were invited to sit around the table with the rest of the family. I remember the father of the young lady telling us that they believed in Jesus; and before we ate, he prayed. It felt like heaven and that young lady definitely was an angel unaware.

Finally, the day came for us to leave the refugee camp. Mutti had heard about a train heading further West. I can't remember the details of how she managed to get us all on the train. We had to get off in the city of Zwickau. The train was now heading in a different direction. Mother asked the official at the train station for direction as to where she might stay with the four of us. But the man was harsh and told her that the city was filled with refugees, and she better find something quick before the curfew began. No wonder Mutti cried out to God for help. As we stepped onto the street, a man pulling a cart passed by us. Mutti asked him for help. He looked at us and told her to follow him. We made it to his home before the curfew. And not only that, but we were invited to come in and occupy a room that had a sofa and a bed. Then, as we sat down for a meager meal, the man explained that they were Christians and prayed before we ate. That was when Mutti started weeping for joy and gratitude. God had again sent His angel to lead us. We stayed with these dear people for a couple of weeks.

Let me tell you…

How We Crossed the Border

Almost five months had passed since we started our flight before the Russian armies. Each day had been a fight for survival. We had no food, no shelter, and now some of us where increasingly sick. Mutti was determined to be home in Luetgendortmund before the cold weather of winter arrived. It was already October 1945. Germany had been divided into four military zones: the Russian, the American, the British and the French. We were still in the Russian zone and needed to go through the American to the British zone. That was where our home was and where we lived before the evacuation to Sudetenland. We dreamed to go back West. Every child seemed to know that the Americans liked children and would even distribute chocolate to them.

Several times, and at different places, mother had tried to cross the border. But it was getting more difficult every time. The Russians were using psychological warfare and making false announcements. They would promise to open the border crossing at a certain place; and when people would rush there, they would deny it and send tanks and soldiers to make them run for cover. I remember how one time my curiosity let me forget to stay close to Mutti. I walked away to inspect one of those tanks. The moment mother saw me, she ran to get me back. A Russian soldier seeing her run came after her. Using his rifle as a club, he missed her by inches as he tried to hit her full force with the rifle butt.

By this time now my 12-month-old sister, Ursula was in bad shape. She was totally undernourished, and Mutti decided to take her to a hospital. She had blue spots over her body and was at times unconscious. The medical personnel insisted Mutti leave her there. Even they weren't sure if they could still help her. Our situation had gotten desperate. It was getting cold, and we just couldn't sleep any longer outside in barns or even pig pens where the Russians had put us sometime. Finding food was becoming more difficult every day. Too many refugees still filled the streets.

One night, after we had again been deceived by false announcements, Mutti knew that we had to cross that border at any price. She explained to Dieter, Marlene and I what we were about to do. She prayed with us and gave us instructions that we had to stay very close. We held hands with each other and followed her in absolute silence as we walked through the dark.

It was raining and cold as we stepped into the night. Before us was an open field that we had to cross before we would come to the border crossing. We heard shots and shouts from the distance. Suddenly, a Russian commanded "Stoy!-zuurueck!" (Stop) in Russian and (go back) in German. Mutti hit us with her body and pushed us against a bush as the flashlight passed by us.

We stood paralyzed in the dark. Then, we heard a voice in high German from close by, "Ist da jemand?" (Anybody there?) Mutti felt safe to identify herself. "Don't go to the left, because the soldiers are drunk and already killed some people. Go to the right." said the voice. We continued now bearing to the right. Suddenly, Mutti disappeared. She had fallen into a foxhole filled with water. With a muffled voice, she called Dieter to hand her the little suitcase he was carrying and to give her his scarf. She tied the scarf to the handle of the suitcase and asked Dieter to hold the end of it while she let the suitcase go down the foxhole. Mutti used the suitcase as a stepping stone and the three of us did the best we could to pull her out.

Then she pulled the suitcase out with the scarf. We continued walking through the mud.

Finally, we were close to the border crossing. To the left, we saw a throng of people standing under a dim street light. The gate was to the right of us, close by in the dark. Soldiers were barking orders. One yelled, "Only children can cross the border." That was our chance. Mutti told us to crawl under the border gate, and she followed with us. Somehow the soldiers didn't pay attention nor see her. Soon, we were walking hand in hand on a small empty road between the Russian and the American border, known as Niemandsland (nobody's land).

We were cold and wet but happy to be walking toward freedom. The first light of dawn started to illuminate the wet street when we arrived at the next border crossing. There was a solitary guard house and another gate. "Crawl under," Mutti encouraged us. As we got up, now on the American side, an apple came rolling toward us. The sentinel, an American soldier, had just started biting into his apple when he saw a woman with her three, small children. We never saw him. But the bitten apple confirmed what we had heard about the Americans. Just an hour earlier, we could have been shot. Now, we were being received with the soldier's apple: a sign of compassion I have never forgotten. Mutti too was deeply moved, and we all rejoiced as we walked toward the little village. We finally had come to freedom. Now, we just needed to find a place where we could dry our wet clothes.

Let me tell you…

How We Made It Home

The apple the American soldier had rolled toward us had an unforgettable impact on me as a 6 year old. What a contrast! An hour earlier, we were risking our lives trying to cross the Russian border and then the American sentinel welcomed us with compassion. In spite of the cold and our wet clothes, his gesture of friendship warmed our hearts and made us breathe a sigh of relief. The perfume of freedom was in the air and in my heart a deep gratitude was born.

Chapter 8

We followed the road and knocked on the door of the first small farmhouse we came to. We were invited in. Other refugees, who had also crossed the border during the night, were there around a fireplace. I remember sitting as close to it as I could and watched the blazing coal. It was so good to be warm and to get dried up again. I remember the barn with fresh straw and the proud rooster, who disturbed by our presence, walked around crowing and scratching the floor. Someone suggested that he would be wonderful for dinner. But someone stole him before the sun was up that next day.

After we dried up and had something to eat, Mutti took us to town to the railway station. I remember being impressed with the American army vehicles painted in a dark green-grayish color with a big white star on the doors. The black soldiers with their shining teeth and happy laughter fascinated me. Wow! Did they ever drive fast!

Mutti was informed that the train was supposed to be leaving that afternoon toward the Ruhrgebiet. That was good news. Soon, we found ourselves in the midst of a sizable crowd waiting for the train to come. As could have been expected, when the train arrived it was already full. It turned into chaos when everybody tried to get on at the same time. Dieter and I were helped by Mutti to climb through a bathroom window. She tried to get on the train through the door, but there was only room for the basket with our few belongings. She ran with Marlene to find space in another wagon, but it too was filled to the brim. The train was already in slow motion when they finally, with the help of others, were able to squeeze through a still open door into a wagon.

Kilometers rolled on as we travelled through bombed out cities and passed destroyed trains. Many of them had a red cross painted on the roof and had been emergency trains for wounded soldiers. It was obvious that the whole railway system was in bad shape because it had been a special target for the allied bombers. Since the shrill whistle of our locomotive had to warn people on the many crossings of our coming, it was blowing all the time. Hour after hour, the train huffed and puffed while the black smoke filled the air with particles of soot.

Dieter and I had to either stand or sit on the floor of that bathroom. There was no space to move. The night was long, and we dozed off a couple of times. It was early morning when the train stopped at a small station. Suddenly, we heard Mutti's voice calling, "Dieter, Edmund come!" But how could we get out? There was no way to go through the people to the door. We had to climb through the bathroom window to the platform again. Mutti helped us. Then, she ran to find her weaved basket. "Help me Lord!" she prayed aloud. She opened the next door, and there it was. As she grabbed it, two other hands were holding it back. But Mutti was in the right, how could she let go? We got the basket just in time as the train was leaving the station.

Now, we were finally in Luetgendortmund. It was still early morning and the place was quiet. As we walked the Hellweg, the same road Napoleon's troops had used in the early 19th century, we saw that many of the houses had been bombarded. What a sinister picture! The bombs had cut through like razor blades. On one wall we could see the bathroom mirror in perfect shape on the second floor, but everything else was gone. Where once the basement had been was now a deep crater.

After we had walked for a mile or so, a girl passed us by on a bicycle. Mutti recognized her. It was Inge Zimny. Her family lived on the same floor where our apartment was. She was so happy to see us after two and a half years since we left for the Sudetenland. As we arrived at our house (#140), we learned that the apartment was not livable. A grenade had exploded right under our window and a lot of repair was needed. Mutti decided to move on to Uncle Hugo's house in Kreta about three miles away. Uncle Hugo was an older brother of my father. We crossed the center of Luetgendortmund which was only partially destroyed. But as we came close to Kreta, the devastation of war was all around us. Uncle Hugo's house had been totally destroyed too and was a heap of rubble. We looked at the back and saw that people were living over the garage. We rang the bell and soon heard a man coughing as he made his way to open the door. It was Uncle Hugo. He looked at us with happy surprise and invited us in. Aunt Aenne and cousin Esther welcomed us too. "Did you hear from Alfred?" asked Mutti. No, there was no news from my dad. Uncle Hugo's son was also missing. How sad! In only a few weeks we were able to move into our old home. We were so thankful that in the meantime our family gave us shelter.

Let me tell you…

About Mutti's Unconditional Love

For a 6 year old, two years makes a big difference. I didn't remember that we had so many wonderful relatives and friends in Ruhrgebiet. One of my father's brothers had a bakery, and another four had butcher shops. Uncle Ernst, who had arrived months earlier, was already employed and had a regular income. He was so glad to see us again.

He told us what had happened the day when he left our home in Teplitz Schoenau after he promised to come back and pick us up before the Russians would come. When he arrived back at the army post, it had already been abandoned. There was no truck left. He kept the small car he was driving, picked up his family and drove west. It was the only direction he could drive since the roads were already clogged with refugees.

A few days after we had come from the east, mother's father Oscar came to see us. He was also the one who fixed our apartment and then decided to come and live with us. We were so happy to have a grandfather whom we called Opa. We knew he would be with us only temporarily since he wanted to return to Brazil as soon as possible. He had come from there just for a visit when Germany started the war in 1939; and he had gotten stuck for six years.

Since the day we left little sister Ursula behind in the hospital in East Germany, Mutti was dreaming about bringing her home. Not for a minute did her heart forget her daughter. Our relatives were united in discouraging her to go back for her. Even Opa was against it. What if Ursula was already dead? Could Mutti justify risking her life for the one that might not be living while her other three children urgently needed their mother? This was not an easy decision to make. Mutti was by nature a peace lover and humble in spirit. She took her father's advice very seriously. But would it be right to sacrifice her mother's heart? In the end, Mutti stood her ground. She had to go and try, even if it meant risking her life. Opa, too, finally gave in and even better, decided to go with her. We children stayed with family during the following weeks and hoped for their safe return.

Mutti had to cross the Russian border again. She and Opa chose the dark of the night and a forest to hide them as they crossed back into East Germany. They made it safely to the hospital and to their amazement found Ursula alive and actually doing much better. They were allowed to take her with them and immediately started planning the dangerous return over the Russian border to the west. Opa had been a decorated soldier in World War I and was a tremendous help and encouragement to Mutti as they had to elude the Russian border guards on their way back.

What a celebration it was when they arrived in Luetgendortmund! Finally, we were together again. In spite of the hard times and little to eat, we did celebrate God's goodness to our family.

Mutti would now concentrate on finding news about my dad's whereabouts. She contacted the Red Cross and other organizations that specialized in discovering what happened to soldiers who had been listed as missing or imprisoned. The newspaper daily published lists of names of those who returned or had been identified as dead. There were all kinds of stories and reports. One time, a certain Fritz X was announced as returning home from prison in Russia. Mother and daughter-in-law went to the train station certain that Fritz Junior, who was missing since the end of World War II, was coming home. But who stepped off the train? It was old and sick father Fritz who, without anybody knowing had been in prison in Russia since WWI. We never heard if his son, Fritz, returned at a later date.

Then, Christmas 1945 arrived. Everyone in our small church family had been touched by the war. Many had lost loved ones, most had lost property and all of them were struggling to make ends meet. We were together in a school building, that was still in need of repair from the damage it had suffered after an air raid, to celebrate the Savior's birth. The Christmas message touched each one in a personal way. Hadn't God sent His Son to be born in poverty to a people living under the rule of foreign military forces? And wasn't the message of the angels one of peace and blessing for people with whom He is pleased? That Christmas, I spoke for the first time in public and quoted a Bible verse. It was 1 John 4:19: "We love because

He first loved us." Yes, God's love made all the difference. The candle light added to the festive mood, and the smell of cookies was an almost unbelievable treat. But over arching all of that was the deep gratitude that filled our hearts because we had our little sister, Ursula, back. God had rewarded Mutti's unconditional love.

Let me tell you...

How God Prepared Us for the Unbelievable

Can siblings be good friends? Just because siblings have the same parents and live in the same house doesn't necessarily mean that they like each other. Friends don't have to be reminded that they should love each other, but we have to be reminded that we should love our enemies. Friends like each other. Well, my sister, Marlene, and I were friends and liked each other very much. When we would walk on the street, we would go hand in hand or even arm in arm. Sometimes when people would smile or snicker at us because we were walking hand in hand we would say, "Well, they don't know what it is when you really like someone." We just loved to be around each other. At 7 years old, I felt like the big brother to my 5-year-old sister, and she was easy to like.

Marlene was special. She was pretty with her dark hair, brown eyes and shy smile. She was mother's comforter when the sadness would set in. During those days, Mutti had so many reasons to worry or to be sad. The daily concern of the whereabouts of my father and the tremendous struggle to survive were reasons enough to be depressed. Mutti had four small children to feed and to cloth, and we were all growing. How could she do it with the meager pension she got from the government? She would take old clothes apart and sew pants, shirts and jackets for us. She would get yarn from old pullovers and crochet socks. Many times, she would work until late in the night. Because of poor nutrition, I was often sick. At one time, they suspected I had tuberculosis; another time, I had jaundice. If it hadn't been for the care packages that my Uncle Oscar from Brazil sent to us via the United States, we would probably have starved to death.

But it wouldn't be correct to say that Mutti was depressed. She loved her Savior, and she loved her children. She knew where to get strength she couldn't muster on her own. She had the habit of playing games with us children and making time for Bible stories, good educational material and missionary biographies. It was fun to be around her.

One Saturday became unforgettable for all of us. As Mutti was reading from a book, suddenly Marlene interrupted and asked her to tell about heaven. Mutti consented and told her some of the information we have from the Bible and added that heaven was so beautiful it was hard to describe. When Marlene asked about the food they ate in heaven, Mutti started wondering. She looked at Marlene and thought, "but you are so pretty and healthy, this is not normal talk for a child like you."

But Marlene didn't stop there. She turned to Dieter and said, "Dieter, you need to accept the Lord Jesus in your heart to be able to go to heaven." And turning to me, she said the same thing adding, "When I will be in heaven, I will take care of Alfredchen." Alfredchen had been our oldest brother who died when he was only 3 years old. Mutti would often tell us of how bright he was and how he loved the stories of Jesus and had such a beautiful singing voice.

The following Monday morning, Marlene had taken Ursula to play outside. In those days, there was almost no traffic on the road, and Mutti could easily watch what was happening from the family room window. So she was not overly concerned as Horst, the neighbor's boy, took Marlene and Ursula across the street to sit on the steps of the restaurant right in front of our house. Horst gave his ball to 2-year-old Ursula. When she let go of it, it rolled across the street.

Now, Horst ordered Marlene to fetch the ball from the other side. She went. As she grabbed the ball and turned to cross the road again, a British army truck, a tank transporter, came flying down the decline at excessive speed. He had turned his engine off and Marlene, who was getting up and turning around, didn't hear or see the truck. The most horrible, unimaginable thing happened. She was hit by the truck and run over by its many wheels. She was killed instantly. The truck had been going so fast it took many yards for it to come to a complete halt.

Mutti was washing dishes when the neighbor knocked on our door. With a pale face and breaking voice told her that something terrible had happened. She shouldn't look out the window. Mutti's heart almost stopped beating as she understood the unimaginable. I can still hear her outcry of pain. I was numb and couldn't process the horrendous happening. Soon, I saw for myself from the other side of the road the gruesome picture I will never forget. Marlene's body was totally crushed. How could our dear Mutti have handled this without the awareness that Marlene was now in the heaven she had longed for? God had prepared her and all of us for the unbelievable tragedy and sustained Mutti in her deepest sorrow.

Let me tell you…
About the Great Discovery

Tears and a terrible sadness had invaded our home. Marlene, Mutti's comforter and my best friend, had been taken from us. If we had at least heard any news about my father, it would have been so much easier for Mutti to endure the pain. Everything had become so dark and hopeless.

It was part of the custom in those days that people would dress in black at the funeral as a sign of respect and solidarity. Many of our family and friends as well as neighbors had come. I heard them whisper in front of the closed casket that because the truck ran over Marlene's body, she was unrecognizable. I knew that. I had seen it. It was indescribable, and I tried not to think of it. It hurt too much. At the service, we sang the beautiful Sunday school songs. The words spoken focused on heaven and the joy Marlene was now experiencing. It was comforting but still a sense of loss and pain shrouded my feelings.

Black now became mother's dress code, and making a visit to the cemetery was a normal routine. I would accompany her most of the time. The grave sites in the huge Luetgendortmunder cemetery were well kept. Mutti insisted that Marlene's grave should also demonstrate our love and care for her. There was a wooden cross with her name, a small star with her birthday, and a small cross with the date she died. She was almost 6 years old. The tomb was under a huge willow tree. Mutti planted flowers and other beautiful plants on it.

At times while she was taking care of the grave, I walked around in between the many tombstones. The area where the crosses for the fallen soldiers were, had special attraction to me. I would read the many names and compare their ages. All had been so young. I would pay attention to their ranks. But what difference did it make. All had to face death. What counted in the end was not what they had been on earth, but rather what they were in God's eyes.

The bombed out cities of the Ruhrgebiet would speak in their own language. One could still read the arrogant slogans on the walls of the train station or other public buildings. "Raeder muessen rollen fuer den Krieg und Koepfe muessen rollen fuer den Sieg! (wheels must turn for the war and heads have to roll for the victory!) What terrible calamity that crooked mentality had brought to the world! Now, all had been touched by the disaster of war. Most people had lost loved ones and all were going through very tough times. The arrogance that had been the hallmark of the Nazi times was now subdued. The cities were a heap of rubble, and it was slowly sinking in that the Hitler regime had been a brutal bunch of liars who had deceived the German people because of their own complex of superiority. Unspeakable crimes and atrocities had been committed.

As spring follows winter, now a time of spiritual awakening followed the political nightmare of World War II. God sent evangelists and preachers to wake up the nation. Werner Heukelback, a simple railroad worker, became one of those messengers of forgiveness, grace and restoration. The Lutheran Nikolai church in the nearby city of Dortmund was filled evening after evening with hundreds of people who came to hear the message of salvation through Jesus Christ. Nobody seemed to care that part of the church building was destroyed. In the afternoon, they had children evangelism, and I went there with friends of ours. My heart was ready. Marlene's challenge for me to accept Jesus was still unanswered. When the invitation was given to pray the prayer of surrender, I confessed to the Lord that I believed that He died for me on the cross, and I asked Him to forgive my sin and to live in my heart.

The joy that entered my soul is impossible to describe. When I went home, I was so happy that I couldn't hold it in. I was singing as I walked through the dark street. "Mutti, I accepted Jesus as my Lord," I blurted out as I entered the kitchen. She gave me a hug and said, "Go, tell Opa!" He was already resting in his room and so I did. God had made me His child. Even at the young age of 7 years old, I knew then and I still know today, that everything I am and I have belongs to the Lord. If Jesus gave His all for me on the cross, how could I ever hold anything back from Him?

After Jesus came into my heart, I wanted everybody to know Him. I would talk with my peers at school about the tremendous discovery I had made. Not everybody was receptive. I experienced the first opposition. But what difference did it make? Actually, the joy of belonging to Jesus became even greater and surer. To know Him is the greatest of all discoveries ever!

Let me tell you…

About a Stormy Night

The years after World War II were very difficult. But I don't remember Mutti ever complaining. She would take her tears and worries to Jesus and explain to us that He who knows and can do everything was watching over us. In spite of all the difficulties, the lack of food, the struggle for proper clothing, and much sickness, I remember my childhood as having been a good one. Mutti would love us with wisdom and entertain us with her creativity. In church, we had good friends who also emphasized family relationships and Christian values. Life lessons were abounding as we often witnessed the adults discussing the deception of the Hitler regime, the unavoidable consequences of sin and pride and then focused on those values money cannot buy.

Materially speaking, we were poor. My shoes were so worn out that my feet would get wet in just a little rain, and we had to walk two miles to school in any weather. My little case that served as a schoolbag holding the slate and a few books would embarrass me many times by just falling apart. We collected old paper and cardboard for recycling so that the school could have books printed for us. I remember one day coming home and part of the plaster from the kitchen ceiling had fallen into mother's biggest cooking pot. The carrot soup she had been cooking was all over the wallpaper. She was sad that we lost the precious food, but she was able to tell us with humor about the "explosion."

In the kitchen, we had a coal oven. But coal was expensive and hard to come by. That's why the day they cut down a tree in the school yard across the street, Mutti got some of the branches for firewood. My brother, Dieter, and I got a cart and started hauling the wood across the street into our cellar. The school was damaged because of the war and had not yet been repaired. The gate instead of being hinged properly was hanging on by rusted wire. For us to get through with our cart, I had to close the gate for Dieter to pass and then open it again for him to be able to get to the street. It worked fine the first time. But at the second passage the disaster happened. The rusted wire broke and the huge gate fell on top of me. I actually can't remember the details, but one spike opened the top of my head. The weight of the gate threw me with such force onto the cobblestone that the base of my cranium broke. At that moment, Dieter had his back to me maneuvering the cart. When he heard the crash, he turned around and saw me lying there unconscious with blood coming out of my nose and ears.

I awoke four days later in the hospital with Mutti at my bedside. The recovery was slow because of the inner bleeding and the extreme concussion my brain had suffered. The doctors told my mother that it was a miracle my reactions were so normal. Thankfully, the whole church was praying. They told me later that people from church would routinely come to the hospital, kneel by my bed in silent prayer and leave again. One day, more than 20 people had visited and prayed. I had to stay in the hospital for six weeks. That was the time I started to understand that God had spared my life for a purpose.

Months later, when I was walking without dizziness, the doctors decided that I should spend time in a recovery house, run by the state health insurance on the island of Norderney. What an adventure! There were 50 other kids my age going as well. We travelled about six hours by train from Dortmund to the harbor city of Norddeich at the North Sea. From there, it took us an hour by ship to the island. What an amazing experience! It was the first time I saw the ocean and smelled the salty sea. I can't describe how impressed I was with the majestic view of the wide horizon and the indescribable quantity of water. I absorbed everything with eagerness. The island had a small town in its center with a beautiful park and a big indoor swimming pool with artificial waves. That was fun! We walked the shore almost every day to collect shells. The harbor was still not totally safe, and it was fascinating to watch the work of the "Minensuchboote" (ships specialized in locating underwater mines).

I remember late one evening while lying in bed in the dark and listening to the howling wind and the braking of the waves at the shore that I was overcome with fear and doubts. What would have happened to me if God had not spared my life? Where would I be? I knew that I was not perfect to merit heaven. But then I thought about the time I asked Jesus to forgive my sin and to come into my heart. Why was I so afraid? It became a real struggle until I jumped out of my bed, knelt down and prayed, "Lord Jesus, I know that you died on the cross for me. I believe you forgave my sin. Please give me peace." And I added, "I will stay on my knees and wait for you to answer my prayer, Amen!" I don't remember for how long I knelt there. Suddenly, in spite of the storm outside all the fear in my heart was gone. Jesus had confirmed His presence in my life. From that day on, I knew the purpose of my life was to serve Him forever. I wanted to become a missionary. This happened in the summer of 1950 when I was 11 years old.